Linkedin Made Easy

By

Linda Parkinson-Hardman

First edition published by: Crystal Clear Books

ISBN: 978-0-9556906-2-4

A catalogue record for this book is available from The British Library.

Telephone: 0843 289 2142
website: www.crystalclearbooks.co.uk

Contents

LINKEDIN MADE EASY

INTRODUCTION

With over 70 million users worldwide representing around 125 different professions, Linkedin is an online social network that seeks to connect people in their PROFESSIONAL capacity. It is very different from many other social networks that you may already have heard about, such as Facebook, because it focuses on our working lives rather than on our social lives.

One way of looking at it, is as an extension of the face to face networking you may do in your local area, when you get together with other business people. However, this is networking on a GRAND scale – how so you might ask?

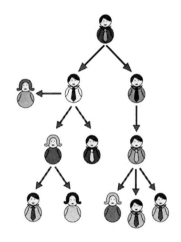

Well, Linkedin allows you to connect to a network of people in three ways. Your 1st degree connections are people you know and they are the centre of your network. Each person connected to one of your direct connections is a 2nd degree connection and those who are linked to your 2nd degree make up your 3rd degree connections. The image explains it a little better than I can.

It uses what we could term, 'friend of a friend' psychology. In other words, I'll recommend this person to you, because I know them and have a relationship with them; in turn we value and respect those recommendations far more than others because there is strong trust element to them.

It enables you to find anyone you have been (or are currently) associated with in a working, business or education environment, because the power of a business lies in its networks of people. In other words, the people that you already know may well be those who are best placed to help you do things like:

- look for a new job
- find out about prospective employees/employers
- research business questions and issues you may have
- provide you with networking opportunities you might not have otherwise
- help you showcase your own expertise, knowledge and skills.

This 'How To' guide is designed to get you started with Linkedin for Business. It will help you to:

- set up an account, if you haven't done so already
- create or rewrite your profile so that you stand out from the crowd
- identify the most appropriate way to use Linkedin for YOU
- work through the fundamentals of designing a strategy for your business use of Linkedin
- Show you how you can use the power of this online powerhouse to grow your business

- Get you started with the various applications that are available.

In short, it will give you a head start over the vast majority of users who simply use Linkedin as a place to post an out of date, inappropriate and pretty pointless CV.

Linkedin offers both free and paid for accounts. The biggest difference is that with a paid account you can send InMails to other users you aren't linked to, which is a great way to reach people not in your network.

 Do bear in mind though, that you don't need a paid account to make the most of Linkedin and there are many ways to expand your network, some of which we'll explore in this guide.

CHAPTER 1 - YOUR BUSINESS STRATEGY

Before you start on Linkedin it's a good idea to have a strategy of some description. Yes, I know, you'd really like to get stuck in connecting with people, improving your profile, demonstrating your many talents and generally throwing some not so sticky mud at walls, hoping it won't slide off before it has a chance to make an impact.

And that's exactly what it will be like if you get started without some idea about what you are trying to achieve, except adding yet another job on the to do list that doesn't provide much in the way of satisfaction.

Any good business strategy starts with an objective, and Linkedin is no different. In fact, if you don't start with an objective then you do risk wasting time you don't have on activities that bear little fruit. However, I have lost count of the number of people (and businesses) I have come across over the years who aren't even really sure what their business does, let alone what their objectives are. I don't mean in the 'we make widgets' or 'we are accountants' sense, I mean in the 'we make others people's lives easier' sense.

Identifying what your business does for other people and businesses is the key to identifying your objectives. Let's say you are a firm of accountants that specialises in the SME (small and medium sized enterprise) market. What is the one statement you might make that would stop someone who is in that market sector in their tracks and cause them to take notice? It might be something as simple as 'fixed monthly fee for freelancers, sole traders and SME's (Small and Medium Sized Enterprises). Why does this matter? Because often they are on tight budgets and it helps to know

5

exactly what is being paid out every month. Of course, you then need to follow that up with the services you offer and why they are appropriate, but you have started on the right foot by getting their attention.

Now that you have the attention – in other words you know what you are doing for other people, you can set the objectives for your business. So, in our fictional accountancy practice that might look something like 'increase the number of monthly billed clients to 20'. It is best to be specific with objectives, because they can then be measured and your activities to achieve them can also be measured.

Setting an objective is often one of the hardest things to do when you are planning any sort of marketing, and to be honest most businesses, large and small, never do it. They rely on the advert in the local paper or directory and the recommendations of their current clients. They hope that someone will miraculously see that they are better than their competitors by osmosis; they don't actively promote their service or their business. Often the reason they don't do anything more than the small advert is because it is perceived as 'selling' and selling is not something that a professional feels they should be doing. So they sit and wait for business to come to them.

According to Ford Harding in his book **Rainmaking**, if you are a professional selling a service, then you can't avoid 'selling' as a fundamental part of your working activity, especially in the current economic climate.

A sales process has five basic stages to it:

1. Be seen by those that are actively seeking your services
2. Identify opportunities and leads
3. Follow up leads

4. Get a meeting or send a pitch

5. Close the sale

Of course, there are many shades of grey in this oversimplified model, and its purpose is simply to highlight the overall actions you need to take. The reason for mentioning it is that networking (whether on or off line) can help you do the first three of these activities quite succinctly, and it will also help you to build great business relationships too.

Once again, according to Ford Harding, there are five specific things you can do that will facilitate all of the above and they are; Article Writing, Public Speaking, Seminars, Publicity and Networking ... and guess what, you can do all of these online and in the social networks.

Linkedin gives you the opportunity to import your articles to your profile, speak publically through group discussions, publicise yourself, your business and your expertise and build a network. The only thing it can't do is give you the opportunity to present to an audience in person, but it will allow you to promote it through events.

Each of these activities could get you to stage 4 of the sales process – getting a meeting or sending a proposal/pitch. After that it's up to you to close the sale.

WHY USE LINKEDIN OVER ANY OTHER NETWORK?

There are many social networks, each catering to a slightly different audience and need. That doesn't mean to say that you can belong to only one, in fact I belong to several and use each of them for business purposes. It's just that the way I use them for business differs significantly because they each have their own unique 'environment' suggesting what is, and isn't acceptable.

I prefer Linkedin to many of the other 'professional' networks for that simple reason, it is more professional. It also happens to be very easy to use and with a few simple tricks and actions you can make it work more effectively.

I mentioned a few reasons to use Linkedin in the introduction and I've included a fuller list here, just to get you thinking:

- Write recommendations for people you know, whose work you have valued
- Display recommendations received from people who like your work
- Demonstrate your expertise by sharing PowerPoint and other presentations on your profile
- Find out who is in town when you are travelling and see if you could meet up
- Create fabulous events with recommended speakers you have found
- List any jobs you have to the whole community
- Similarly, look to see who is recruiting and research companies before you apply
- Find contractors and product/service providers by asking your network
- Use polls for quick and simple market research
- Answer questions and consequently demonstrate expertise without a hint of self-promotion
- Ask questions to get the latest industry perspective or thinking

- Publish your own, unique Linkedin web address on all of your marketing literature
- Use your status updates as a way to showcase your current projects
- Use status updates to share information, articles and resources that you have found particularly helpful
- Connect with like-minded fellows who share common passions and aims in Linkedin Groups.

Mostly, the list of things above that you can use Linkedin to do, fall into one of four camps:

- Marketing – your business, products, services or even yourself
- Research – market or professional development
- Personal Brand Building – to create a more dynamic, visible profile as an 'expert'
- Support – for your customers, your peers and your network.

However, what you may have felt when presented with the list above is something along the lines of *"what, you want me to do all that? When am I going to find the time and how am I going to do it?"*.

The trick is to start with one of the four camps listed above; decide what your overall objective will be for Linkedin. For instance, something like *'develop my awareness of social marketing'* or *'build a network of contacts I can collaborate on larger projects with'* will help you to direct your energy and time in a more focused way.

Each of the activities will quite happily stand alone; you don't have to do all of them or even some of them. Just one of them could be enough to get you to that stage 4 of the sales process. But, as in life, the more you can do the better, because you are giving yourself the best possible chance of being 'seen' by the right person at the right time in accordance with that objective you've already set yourself.

In fact, why don't you write down your initial objective for your business or your career in the box below?

My objective is:

Once you have your overall objective, you can then think about how you are going to achieve that objective. This is the time to start employing some blue sky thinking and perhaps get the help of your colleagues, employees and friends. The process of identifying how to work with an objective is as follows:-

- Establish the goal and make it SMART (specific, measurable, achievable, realistic and timed). It must be something that can be measured, rather than a woolly statement that means nothing (rather like most corporate mission statements!)

- Ask everyone to contribute ideas as to how that objective could be achieved without discussion or criticism – you don't know at this stage just what might be effective
- Group them into categories and then discuss which ones are, in fact, realistic. For instance, saying that talking to the Prime Minister about your problem might not be realistic, but sending a letter to the appropriate Government Minister and requesting a 'surgery meeting' with your local MP just might
- Break the groups down into actions that are each measurable and achievable
- Give one person the responsibility of managing each action with an overall person coordinating effort.

Let's take that objective of increasing the number of SME clients to 20. The actions you might take could include:

- Talking to your current clients about the service you provide to find out why they think you are the best thing since sliced bread.
- Asking for testimonials about the service you provide
- Breaking the comments down into sales hooks – that capture people's attention
- Committing to networking both on and off line to build up your profile
- Getting a better understanding of the factors that are affecting SME's currently

I hope you get the picture. Your major objective can be broken down into smaller and smaller elements, each one is more easily achieved because it requires less input and work, but collectively they have a great impact. There is truth in saying 'The whole is greater than the sum of the parts'. Below, I've created a list of a few actions you might decide to take on Linkedin when you are looking at just 'committing to networking'.

1. Add the people you already work with collaboratively to your network.

2. Have a look at who people in your current network know and who they might be able to introduce you to.

3. Use the search facility on Linkedin to find others with the same or complimentary skills that you might need and send them a message asking them if they would be interested in connecting.

4. Read people's profiles and watch their online activities to determine whether they really do know what they are talking about.

5. Find two groups that reflect the market sector you work in and see if there is any discussion taking place that you can get involved in.

6. Start a discussion on one of the groups yourself about the area you are interested in and respond to replies and comments.

7. Asking a question like "can anyone recommend a person in this field?" or "how can I develop a particular service further?" could be good starting points.

8. Add services or business needs to your current status and ask for people to get in touch.

9. Mention your services, skills and knowledge in your summary so that you show up on other people's searches.

Already in this one area you are able to start the process of finding out what people need, what people want, what your customers think about you and display their testimonials, just in one single social network. Imagine if that were replicated across multiple social and face to face networks. And I'll bet it doesn't feel like selling either.

Chapter 12 contains a number of simple 'recipes' you could follow for a variety of different objectives and situations.

Now that I've given you a few ideas, why not have a go at writing some of your own. Don't worry about *how* you might do these things for the time being as I'll take you through those steps in the rest of this book. For now, all that matters is that you have something specific to focus on.

To achieve my objective I could:

That's great, now you have something to focus on and we can get started with using Linkedin properly.

If you have an account you can skip the next chapter, although it might be helpful to review the information if you are new to the network too. If you don't, this is where you get started.

CHAPTER 2 - CREATING AN ACCOUNT

Creating an account on Linkedin is relatively straightforward and starts at the Linkedin home page.

www.Linkedin.com

When you visit Linkedin, this is what you will see when you get there:

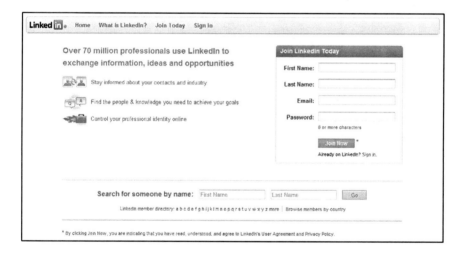

Step 1

Once you have added your First Name, Last Name, Email Address and your chosen Password (don't forget to write your password down!) and clicked on the Join Now button; you will be redirected to a page that asks you whether you are employed, a business owner, working independently,

15

looking for work or a student.   You need to pick the one that matches your CURRENT state most accurately.

Step 2

In the following columns, you will see the questions that are asked depending on the employment (or otherwise) state that you choose.

Employed	Company (Name)	
	Job Title	
	Country	
	Postal Code	
A Business Owner	Company (Name)	
	Industry (Sector)	From a drop down list
	Country	
	Postal Code	
Looking for Work	Industry (Sector)	From a drop down list
	Country	
	Postal Code	
Working Independently	Industry (Sector)	From a drop down list
	Country	
	Postal Code	
A Student	Education (Country)	From a drop down list
	Dates You Attended	From a drop down list
	Field of Interest (Sector)	From a drop down list
	Country	
	Postal Code	

Step 3

Once you have completed step 2, you will be taken to the next page (Step 3) where you can import the email addresses of your current contacts if you use one of the following services: Yahoo!, Gmail, AOL or Hotmail.

16

Don't forget though, that you will need to share your username and password for these accounts with Linkedin so that it can retrieve the information it needs to work with and you may not want to do that.

 If you don't want to do this, use the handy "Skip This Step" link that appears underneath the box to the right.

Step 4

Once you have completed the sign up process, you will be asked to confirm your identify by proving that your email address is genuine. This is common practice online and is just one of the ways in which organisations try to filter out spam and malicious users.

Of course, this is the point where you worry that you may have got it wrong ☺. You should receive an email that looks something like the one on the next page.

Can you see the very first sentence that says "**CLICK HERE to confirm your email address**"? You now need to click on it, or copy the full link given below it, into your web browser (Internet Explorer, Firefox or whichever you prefer) and press the return key on your keyboard.

This will confirm to Linkedin that your email address is genuine and not just a robot trying to create false (spam) accounts.

Once you have clicked, you will be asked to confirm it's you by logging in with the email address you used AND the password you wrote down (Remember!).

LinkedIn

Click here to confirm your email address.

If the above link does not work, you can paste the following address into your browser:

https://www.linkedin.com/e/cnf/rD8YHflY3XOqTCudr4Q1kORtyNwX71pjAShD/

You will be asked to log into your account to confirm this email address. Be sure to log in with your current primary email address.

We ask you to confirm your email address before sending invitations or requesting contacts at LinkedIn. You can have several email addresses, but one will need to be confirmed at all times to use the system.

If you have more than one email address, you can choose one to be your **primary email address**. This is the address you will log in with, and the address to which we will deliver all email messages regarding invitations and requests, and other system mail.

Thank you for using LinkedIn!

--The LinkedIn Team
http://www.linkedin.com/

@ 2009, LinkedIn Corporation

That's it; your account at Linkedin is created. Now all you have to do is use it correctly, and that's the subject for the rest of this guide.

CHAPTER 3 - GETTING STARTED

The very first time you login to Linkedin, you'll be presented with a build your network box that suggests you start using your current contacts, it's very similar to the questions that were being asked when you first signed up.

When you login after you have started to build your network you will see something like the image on the next page. This is your Linkedin home page and you will come into this section of the site every time you start a session on the network.

Your Linkedin home page is unique to your account, so you will only see the things that are happening with YOUR network. As you scroll down this page you will see that the page is divided into two halves with the following sections:

Left hand side
- Your Inbox, the emails you have received as well as a tab showing any new invitations to connect.
- Your Network Activity. At the top is a box where you can add your status update, and below is a stream of the most recent activity from everyone in your immediate network and it will typically show about 15 items – although this will depend on the size of your network and the amount of activity it's members undertakes. There is a link to See More Network Updates right at the end of the stream.

- Your Group Updates will show the most recent three items for each of the top three groups (according to levels of activity) that you are a member of.
- Just Joined Linkedin at the very end will show you those organisations you have listed somewhere in your profile so that you can see if anyone new has joined recently that you might want to connect up with.

Right hand side

- **People you may know** is determined by the other people you are connected to on Linkedin and it will change randomly every time you load this page.
- An advert, usually for one of the Linkedin partners

- **Who's viewed my profile** (See Next Page) gives you the most recent viewings of your profile in the last three days. If you click on the link it will take you to a page similar to the one below and you can follow each of those links and try to work out who it is (unless a specific name has been given).
- The statistics for YOUR Linkedin network across ALL your three network levels.
- The latest information from any of the Applications you are using. You can find out more about Applications in Chapter 11. There are 16 applications currently, with more being added regularly.

On my home page, I'm using:
- Reading list by Amazon
- Events
- Slideshare
- Company Buzz
- Polls
- Wordpress
- My Travel
- Tweets
- Google Presentation

The advantage of having a home page that displays in this way is because it allows you to see at a glance what the most recent activity is. Giving you a quick overview of what's hot and what's trending.

Who's Viewed My Profile

Your profile has been viewed by **8 people** in the last **3 days**, including:

Someone in the Consulting function in the Textiles industry

Someone in the Executive Leadership function in the Marketing and Advertising industry from Bournemouth, United Kingdom

Someone in the Leadership function in the Management Consulting industry from Coventry, United Kingdom

Someone in the Security and Investigations industry from Dorchester, United Kingdom

Manager at Action for Children

██████████ Someone from Contract/Freelance

Partner at Weightmans

███████████████, Someone from Rishabh Software Pvt. Ltd.

CHAPTER 4 - BUILDING & IMPROVING YOUR PROFILE

If you click on 'Profile' in the top navigation bar, it will bring you to the most important part of your Linkedin experience. This is where other people will go to see what you are about, who you are and what your skills, knowledge and specialities are.

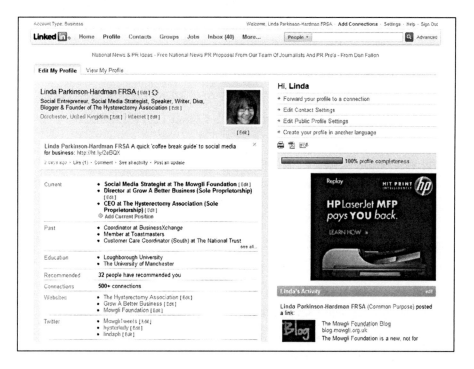

If you don't have a complete profile then you will be missing out on vital opportunities for you, your business or career.

When you start out, your profile will be about 25% complete. Your aim is to get to 100% and to do that you will need to add the following items:

Add a position	+ 15%
Add your education	+ 15%
Add a picture	+ 15%
Add your summary	+ 15%
Add your specialities	+ 5%
Ask for a recommendation	+ 5%

But, astute readers will have noticed that this does NOT add up to 100%

So, what do you need to do to get to 100% on a Linkedin profile? Well, according to Linkedin, adding **TWO PAST POSITIONS** and **THREE RECOMMENDATIONS** will give you a **COMPLETE** Profile.

Also according to Linkedin, those who have a **COMPLETE** profile are 40% more likely to receive opportunities too. So it's worth getting it done sooner, rather than later.

The next page shows '*one I created earlier*' as an example of how NOT to do a Linkedin profile!

This person has made some classic mistakes in their profile (and by the way, this is based on an actual person, but names and details have been changed to protect the innocent).

Problem Areas

Her profile is not complete – just have a look back at the previous chapter to see what's missing.

1. She has a sum total of TWO connections. In any social network, it's your connections that make it worthwhile doing and frankly two isn't worth bothering with.

2. She doesn't even list a website. What about including the name of the website or the web address to give people a clue. On my profile I have listed three out of my four websites, and the only reason I don't have the other one included is because you are limited to three!

3. There is **NO** summary or list of specialities. This can be one of the biggest mistakes people make BECAUSE they assume that Linkedin is just an online CV. What you put in your summary, and in your specialities, can be indexed by search engines like Google. Forget to do it at your peril ……. You have been warned!

4. Unfortunately, she follows this lack with one that is almost as bad, which is not expanding on her experience.

5. She has not asked either of her TWO connections for a recommendation which means that no one can see if she can actually do what she says she can, without having to ask them.

6. Finally, there is no additional information which shows that she is actually a real person, and she hasn't joined any of the many groups that are available.

Here is my list of **TOP TEN THINGS TO CONSIDER** when writing or updating a profile on Linkedin:

1. As with any news story, the first thing seen needs to describe **YOU**, in your own voice. You could even consider asking a question in your heading – this can be intriguing to readers.

2. Ask for recommendations from colleagues, clients and others that know you well.

3. When you add your website addresses, don't forget to use them in the link. Too often they say 'my website' rather something infinitely more informative which is the actual web address.

4. Your summary is the equivalent of your 1 minute elevator speech. It should say who you are and what you do – not the specifics, but how you enable others to gain the best from their business. Therefore, you don't say 'I sell cars'; you say 'I get people from A to B faster'. It is also appropriate to add your goals in here too.

5. Don't forget your specialities too – these are key words and phrases that describe your skills, knowledge and experience and can be used to find people like you easily.

6. Explain the context of your experience – many people won't know what ABC Widgets Ltd do or did.

7. Explain the context of your education as well, especially if it's relevant to what you are doing now.

8. Use the additional information section. Linkedin is about people and relationships, therefore, show your readers that you are, in fact, a real person. But, don't go overboard, this isn't Facebook, so it doesn't require a warts and all exposé.

9. Add a good, professional picture of yourself, people like to see who they are 'talking' to and you'd be surprised at the number of people who remember the name, but can't just bring you to mind.

10. Finally, update your contact settings to let people know what you are interested in.

 You can see my profile by typing in this web address: www.linkedin.com/in/lindaph

Exercise

Before you get started on your new profile it might be worth reviewing the following questions as well as your past positions first; this is because you will have skills, knowledge and experience that are as relevant today as they were in the past and it is worth highlighting them; you never know why someone will want to connect with you or work with you and one of these could be the key element.

1. What are the elements of the role that are relevant in my current position?
2. What were the goals I set myself and did I meet them?
3. What are my personal goals now?
4. How do my personal goals match my objectives for my business or career?

The picture on the next page shows you just how powerful a network can be. However, one thing to bear in mind is that if everyone you are connected to also has only a few connections, then your network will be much smaller.

The statistics on the next page show the number of people I'm connected to directly, as well as through the groups I'm a member of and the people who are connected to my connections.

Your Network of Trusted Professionals

You are at the center of your network. Your connections can introduce you to 9,395,000+ professionals — here's how your network breaks down:

1	**Your Connections** Your trusted friends and colleagues	596
2	**Two degrees away** Friends of friends; each connected to one of your connections	**236,700+**
3	**Three degrees away** Reach these users through a friend and one of their friends	**9,157,700+**
	Total users you can contact through an Introduction	**9,395,000+**

13,737 new people in your network since July 22

CHAPTER 5 - SETTING THE SETTINGS

The settings function on Linkedin controls the vast majority of what people, both on and off the network can see. They also help to control what activities you are alerted to and which ones you ignore.

Some of the settings that are specifically for things like groups will be covered in Chapter 8 so for the time being we are going to concern ourselves only with what you might want other people to see about your activity.

Your settings can be controlled from different locations. Both of these places control similar settings, it's just that from the top menu bar, you access everything in one place and from your profile you are controlling just what people can see and what can be indexed by external search engines.

You can access your settings from the top menu bar as below:

or from your edit profile page on the left hand side of the screen. There are additional ways to access the various settings for each element of Linkedin too, but I'll cover those as we come to them.

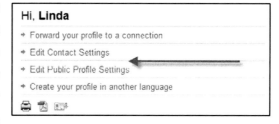

Why would I want to control my settings?

You may well be asking yourself the question, why is it important to control the settings on your account? A good example of having rigid settings preventing indexing and random viewing might be someone who is looking for employment but doesn't want their employer to know.

However, the vast majority of users of Linkedin will be actively seeking to promote themselves, their business and/or their career. Therefore being aware about what you could, and should, change is always well worth doing.

YOUR PUBLIC PROFILE

This is the place most people will want to start with when it comes to knowing what others might see or have access to. When you click on the link to Edit Public Profile Settings, you are presented with two options, the first is to change your public profile URL (which is covered at the end of this chapter) and the second is to amend the list of options shown on the right hand side.

You can see that on my profile (next page), I have selected to have a Full View – this means that my profile is indexed by the likes of Google and Yahoo! and if I were to search for myself on those search engines, then my Linkedin profile would almost certainly be towards the top (if not at the top) of the listings.

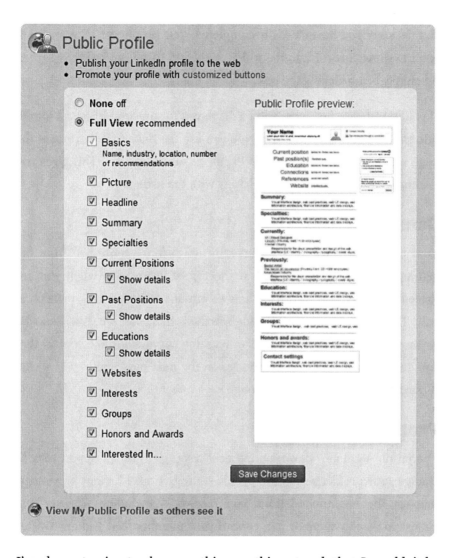

I'm also not going to share anything on this network that I wouldn't be happy for anyone to know, it is already public knowledge in the most part and therefore exposure to the greatest number of people is in my interests as a business consultant.

But, let's say you haven't really completed your profile yet. You may not want to show parts of it to the wider world and those can be easily turned off simply be un-ticking the box.

If you want to see just what will be displayed to someone who isn't logged into the Linkedin network, then you can use the link at the bottom of the page which says 'View My Public Profile as others see it'. This gives you the chance to check that you are happy with the listing.

GENERAL SETTINGS

Your general settings for the Linkedin network are controlled from the settings link that you can find at the top of every page when you are logged in. This page gives you lots of options to check and uncheck at will. From here you can determine whether others can see your contacts, if you want to participate in market research surveys and the contact that you are happy to receive. The image on the next page shows you all the different options and I'll talk through each one it turn.

PROFILE SETTINGS

The profile settings (shown on the next page) give you an opportunity to change your profile, access the profile settings I talked about previously, manage the recommendations you receive – including whether you choose to display them or not, control your member feed and any twitter accounts you may have.

Your member feed is what governs the information and activities that appear on other people's home pages. I have mine set to everyone, because I want the widest possible exposure for my online business activities.

You can add as many twitter accounts as you have, I have two *@lindaph*, and also *@hysterlady*. However only one will be my primary twitter account and this is the one that I would send Linkedin status updates out from if I had turned that on.

You may have noticed that people work with twitter in two ways on Linkedin. The first is that their status updates are broadcast to their twitter account automatically. The second is that some people have twitter updating their Linkedin status update. Personally, I don't do the latter because my 'tweets' are not necessarily appropriate in this context. You will need to take a view on that and it is in this area that you can control how Linkedin and twitter work together.

Personal Information

These settings determine how much personal information can be seen about you and your main account details. It is here that you would go to if you decided to close your Linkedin account or if you had accidentally created multiple profiles.

Email Notifications

Do you want to receive emails from the people that are connected to you and from those who might like to connect to you? I'd be surprised if the answer here were '*no*', after all this is a networking organisation where the objective is to meet people.

You may, though, have a perfectly good reason why you don't want the world and his wife contacting you and it is in this section of settings that you can control what does and doesn't happen. It is also here that you can turn off the emails that come from advertisers on the Linkedin network.

Settings

Profile Settings

My Profile
Update career and education, add associations and awards, and list specialties and interests.

My Profile Photo
Your profile photo is visible to **everyone.**

Public Profile
Your public profile displays **full** profile information.
http://uk.linkedin.com/in/lindaph

Manage Recommendations
You have received 32 recommendations
27 clients, 5 partners

Member Feed Visibility
Your member feed is visible to **everyone.**

Twitter Settings
Add your Twitter account on your profile.

Email Notifications

Contact Settings
You are receiving **Introductions, InMails, and OpenLink Messages.**

Receiving Messages
Control how you receive emails and notifications.

Invitation Filtering
You are receiving **all invitations.**

Partner InMails
Control how you receive informational and promotional messages from LinkedIn's marketing and hiring partners.

Home Page Settings

Network Updates
Settings for the display of Network Updates on your home page.

RSS Settings

Your Private RSS Feeds
Enable or disable your private RSS feeds.

Groups

Group Invitation Filtering
You **are receiving** Groups Invitations.

My Groups
Settings for groups you manage or belong to.

Groups Order and Display
Choose which groups display in what order in the main navigation.

Personal Information

Name & Location
Control your name, location, display name, and account holder icon display settings.

Email Addresses
Your primary email address is currently:
linda@growabetterbusiness.co.uk

Change Password
Change your LinkedIn account password.

Close Your Account
Disable your account and remove your profile.

Privacy Settings

Research Surveys
Settings for receiving requests to participate in market research surveys related to your professional expertise.

Connections Browse
Your connections are **not allowed** to view your connections list.

Profile Views
Control what (if anything) is shown to LinkedIn users whose profile you have viewed.

Viewing Profile Photos
You can view **everyone's** profile photos.

Profile and Status Updates
Control whether your connections are notified when you update your status or make significant changes to your profile and whether those changes appear on your company's profile.

Service Provider Directory
If you are recommended as a service provider, you **will** be listed.

NYTimes.com Customization
Control the LinkedIn-integrated headline customization and enhanced advertising on NYTimes.com.

Partner Advertising
Control whether you will be shown LinkedIn Audience Network advertisements on partner websites.

Authorized Applications
See a list of websites or applications you have granted access to your account and control that access.

My Network

Using Your Network
Tell us how you want to use your LinkedIn network.

Privacy Settings

You can choose how others view your data with a whole range of privacy settings. For instance, I have chosen not to allow my list of connections to be visible to everyone simply because I'm what is called an 'open networker' (more about that later) and I know that some people have connected to me simply to see who I'm connected to and gain access to them.

This is also where I control what other people will see if I go and have a look at their profiles. Remember, in Chapter 3 where we saw the 'Who's viewed my profile' tab on our home page? Well this is how people control what can be seen. Personally, I'm quite happy for people to know I've visited them, but you may have a very good reason not to do that.

Home Page Settings

Your home page settings give you the option to change what is displayed on your home page, or not, as the case may be.

If you want a quick overview of the activity of your network it is probably best to leave the settings as they are. If you want to see only those areas (or people) you are specifically interested in, then this is the place to create that specific view.

RSS Settings

RSS means many different things, but the most popular is *Really Simple Syndication*. What this means is that whenever you (or your network undertakes an action on Linkedin) that this is broadcast to a 'news reader' of your/their choice, so that you don't have to be connected to Linkedin permanently to find out what's going on in your network.

Groups

This is where you can manage how the list of groups you belong to is displayed on the Groups Home Page. If you have a lot, but only visit a few on a regular basis, you may want to move them to the top of the page!

CREATE A PERSONALISED LINKEDIN URL FOR YOUR PROFILE:

Remember at the end of the last chapter, I offered you the opportunity to have a look at my profile? Well, you may have noticed something different about my profile web address compared to yours. That's because I have created a personalised Linkedin Public Profile URL and here's how you can do it too.

1. Click on Profile in the top navigation bar menu.
2. Click on Edit Public Profile Settings.
3. The first thing you will see is a statement in bold that says "**Your Public Profile URL**" with an *edit* button next to it.
4. When you click on that 'edit' button you will get a form that looks like this and you can simply give yourself a new moniker.

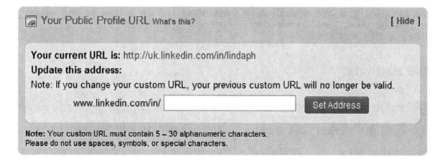

CHAPTER 6 - CREATE A STRATEGY FOR CONNECTIONS

Some of you will already have a number of connections on Linkedin, and others won't have any. However, it is important that you determine what your connection strategy is going to be, otherwise it can be 'just so much mud' slung at walls hoping that some will stick.

The most important thing that you need to ask when considering connections is "what am I hoping that Linkedin will do for me?"

The reason we talk about 'me', rather than 'my business', is because Linkedin, as a social network, is essentially about individuals rather than businesses, and reflects who and what they know. The key is that word 'social', as this is about building relationships.

It is the place where you are able to demonstrate your expertise in a given area and where you can showcase your projects, talents, knowledge and skills. Your business, if you have one, or the company you work for are a **PART** of who **YOU** are, not the **WHOLE** of who you are.

Therefore, your use of this particular social network should really be about driving attention towards **YOU**.

At the last count, there were over 70 million professionals with a profile on Linkedin. However, not all of those profiles will be current, and not everyone you meet online will be the right sort of person you want to link with.

Have a think about the following questions and see if you can answer them:

1. Would you like to link only with people you know? This is the route that is recommended by Linkedin. And is a good policy to follow, because networking, on or offline is all about the relationship you develop with the people you know.

2. Are there any actions you can take that facilitate the start of a relationship? For instance, I often ask the people who answer my questions to connect with me if it seems we have something in common.

3. Are you prepared to be a LION? A LION is a Linkedin Open Networker. These are people who are prepared to link to people they don't know to open up networks that may be closed otherwise. I will link to people I don't know, but I make sure I check them out first by reading their profile and any recommendations to see if they are an appropriate 'fit'. In other words, are they interested in the same things I'm interested in, or are they just trying to get to my network of contacts?

4. Is your business B2B (business focused) or is it B2C (consumer focused)? If it is the latter, then it may be worth using Linkedin to look for collaborations, undertake continuing professional development or even provide help and support to other, related, industries in your market sector.

5. Who in your audience uses Linkedin? For instance, as CEO of The Hysterectomy Association, I know that if any members are using

this social network they probably wouldn't want their work colleagues making assumptions about their health issues.

6. Would you be prepared to link to past or current employers or employees? Think about this one carefully, because they will know things about you that you might not wish to be made public in the present day.

7. Is it appropriate to link to all your customers, clients and suppliers? One suggestion is to only link to those who might recognise your name.

8. What about people you might meet whilst out networking in the real world? I often send a request to join me on Linkedin when I have met someone to talk to at a business event, but only if they gave me their card. It also means I don't have to store the card any longer either.

Once you have some appropriate answers to the questions above, then it's time to get started with some work on increasing your connections. But first, a few does and don'ts before you begin putting your strategy into place:

Don't spam – in other words, don't come to Linkedin hoping to sell your wares. This is a place to network and although business happens within it, people actually want to focus on developing a relationship with you, not listen to a 'pitch'. You will turn them off pretty quickly otherwise.

Don't forget who might see your profile – remember some of it may be visible with a very basic Google search for your name. In fact, why not go along to Google now and see if you can find yourself, I'll bet your Linkedin profile comes up pretty high on the list if you've been a member for any length of time.

Don't send out canned invitations – there is a reason why there is a link to *EDIT/PREVIEW INVITATION TEXT*. By using it, and writing something personal in the message, people will be more likely to remember you and want to link with you – because you are demonstrating that you **KNOW** something about them and are therefore interested in **THEM** and not just their connections.

Don't preach to the converted – in other words, if someone you are asking to become a connection is already listed on Linkedin, there is no need to tell them about the benefits of being on the site, they already know that and either use it, or not.

Don't get upset when people don't accept your invitation – it may be that they have their own connection strategy in place that doesn't include the group of people you are in; or it may be that they don't want to use the site.

HOW TO REQUEST A CONNECTION

1. After logging in to your account, click on **contacts** in the top navigation menu.
2. Next click on **Add Connection** – you can see it in the right hand top corner of the image on the previous page.
3. The image below shows you **THREE** options, you don't have to choose just one, you can use all three. You can add connections manually either by individual email address or through an email

account you have; you can find colleagues you already know or
you can find classmates you were at college or university with.

4. The final option, People You May Know is the same as the
   function that presents three people on your home page and these
   are people connected to other contacts you may already have.
   Personally, I never import my contacts from Outlook, and I don't
   have a webmail account either. This is just my preference, and if
   you have an extensive list of people on your email account who
   you would like to connect with, then do use the options presented
   to you on the left hand box above.

If you are an employee of a large organisation currently, then choosing
the second tab is always worthwhile as it may flag up people you already
know who are also listing the organisation in their profiles. The same is
true for Classmates too.

However, my preference is the box on the right hand side. This gives me
the option of typing in their email address and then use the link
immediately below it that says "Add a personal note to your invitation"
where I can change the canned message.

43

There is an alternative way to add a connection to your contacts list which works with other people who are on Linkedin already.

1. You can use the search facility that you will see in the top right hand part of the Linkedin screen to find people already listed on the network. The image overleaf shows you the type of result you might get if you searched for me, Linda Parkinson-Hardman.

2. If you have a list of results for names that are slightly more common, you will see that Linkedin have provided a handy advanced search facility on the left hand side of the page which allows you to segment results by a variety of different factors, including: company details, location, relationships, industry, education and groups.

3. As you hover over the individuals details they will turn blue and you will see a link that says *"Add to network"*.

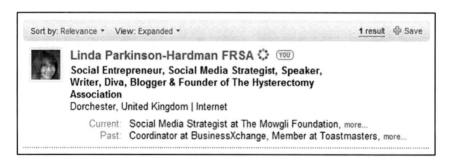

4. You will have to indicate how you know the person you are contacting, and in some instances you will also need to know their email address. You will be presented with a number of options. These are: Colleague, Classmate, We've done business together, Friend, Other, I don't know XYZ. Unsurprisingly, if you choose the last option you won't get any further.

As you build your network on Linkedin, you'll be able to check your network statistics regularly to see how you are doing and where your network is currently located. You can find your detailed information about YOUR network statistics by clicking on the link to **Network Statistics**, which is located in the drop down menu underneath **Contacts** in the top navigation bar.

 Don't forget that personal note; it really does make all the difference.

GETTING CONNECTED EXERCISE

Now that you understand the fundamentals, it is important to think through your strategy BEFORE taking any action. Answering the following questions should help you clarify your aims and objectives.

1. Would you like to link only with people you know? If so, why?
2. Are you prepared to be a LION?
3. Is your business B2B or is it B2C? Does this matter if your consumer audience are professionals for instance?
4. Who in your audience uses Linkedin? Are there any things you need to take into account?
5. Would you be prepared to link to past or current employers or employees? If not, why not?
6. Is it appropriate to link to all your customers, clients and suppliers? Are there some you might not want to link to and why?

7. What about people you might meet whilst out networking? What do you already do with their business cards, if anything?

Remember, there is ONE golden rule, **NEVER, EVER use the IDK (I don't know) link** when you receive a request from someone else you don't want to link to. Doing so can harm their standing on Linkedin and **YOU** only need to archive or delete the request to ignore it.

CHAPTER 7 - MANAGING YOUR CONNECTIONS

How often are you given a business card? Is it daily, weekly, monthly? Do you get them at every networking event you attend or pick them up from the counter of local suppliers you use?

I have gathered hundreds over the years and I know people who gather thousands. The sad truth is that if someone doesn't do something with a business card they've received straight away, then it will either be consigned to the bin or to a 'storage' facility and destined never to see the light of day again.

Some people have decided that the way to manage this information overload is to use a spreadsheet or a contact management system or even Outlook. The problem they find though is that they still have to:

a. Remember the person that they want to speak to so they can find them again

b. Actively do something to keep in touch

But what if you could have a system that would keep all your business contacts in one easy to find place that would prompt you every time someone you knew was doing something of interest and also allowed you to share information and have a conversation in a single click of mouse button.

Linkedin offers you a fantastic opportunity to manage all those business details in one easy place, with the added facility that you can quickly and easily catch up with any one of the people you have met over the years.

You can find such a system when you click on Contacts in the top menu bar.

The contacts tab provides you with easy access to everything you need to add and manage contacts. This is also where you will find those interesting network statistics, that detail how many people you can actually reach at the first, second and third level of your network.

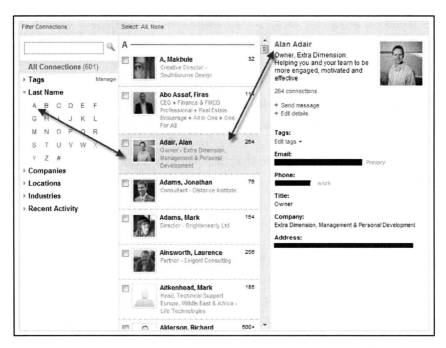

For now though we are only interested in My Connections which is the first page you come to when you click on the Contacts tab. This is the place that lists your contacts alphabetically.

You will notice that on the left hand side of the screen, there are a number of ways that have automatically been provided that allow you to filter your contacts. These include:-

- Filters such as TAGS, which include people you share a common group with, people you have connected with because they are friends or even people who are your partners in a business.

- Filters for last name, company, location, industry and recent activity.

You are also able to see your most recent connections – usually those you have connected to within the last seven days, this is useful so that you can quickly follow up by sending a message to them to say 'hello'.

Finally, there is a link that shows you the connections you have that also have new connections, this is a great way to find out if there is anyone else you should be linking up with.

There are three columns in the contact organiser. The left hand column is the filter column as described above, the middle column lists all your contacts in alphabetical order and the final column is normally blank. This is the column that is used by Linkedin to display one of two things:

- The contact details of a specific contact that you have selected from your contact list
- The link to send a message to a group of contacts you have selected by using a filter.

The example on the previous page shows you the results that I have found when I selected the contacts with last names beginning with A and then the single contact, Alan Adair, that I was looking for in this instance. I now have FIVE options,

- I can have a look at Alan's connections (because he has allowed his contacts to see them)
- send him a message
- edit the details I have for him
- choose the tags I want to be able to find him under
- send him an email

The details that I see for Alan are only those are listed on his profile, but as I get more information about him I will be able to add it to MY information about him. This won't be shown publically and is only ever going to be available to me.

This ability to edit contacts is what allows Linkedin to become a pretty good contact management system.

I can now add information such as extra email addresses, phone numbers, websites, birthdays, contact notes and instant message services. You can see at the bottom of the page a small asterisked item that says 'information you've added', this is to distinguish it from information Alan adds to his profile.

IMPORTED CONTACTS

I know that one of the questions you may have is that this is all very well, but what about those business cards I've got stored away for people that aren't on Linkedin yet?

That's the beauty of this system; Linkedin gives you the opportunity to import a contact list from any other system you use currently in the form of a CSV, TXT or VCF file. This means that anyone you currently have stored in something like Outlook could be added to your Linkedin account, even though they aren't on the Linkedin network themselves.

Once they add themselves to the network, their name in your Imported Contacts section will change colour to **Blue** and a little **IN** icon will be presented that shows they have now added a profile, and you can then follow up with a connection request if you would like to.

In the meantime, all of the information you have about that person is stored on Linkedin and you can easily send them an email right from within your Imported Contacts list.

PROFILE ORGANISER

In this book, I have tried to avoid talking about any of the premium features that a paid account will provide on Linkedin. The reason for this is because the vast majority of features are available to the free user. However, there is one benefit that may make it worth considering buying a professional subscription for and that is the Profile Organiser.

The Profile Organiser is what turns Linkedin into a fully functional Contact Management System that allows you to:-

- add contacts to folders you create
- add prospects (people you aren't connected to at all) to folders
- create notes for those people on a regular basis

In short it allows me to keep a list of those people I am specifically working with or targeting in a handy list that is segmented to meet my needs. I can watch what they are doing on Linkedin to see if there is an opportunity for me to contact them or keep in touch; I can find references for them by searching the network and I can follow up on work we are already doing.

I have folders for current clients, past clients, for local businesses and for my top prospects. I may choose to create any number of other folders too, depending on changes to my business strategy in the future.

CHAPTER 8 - LINKEDIN GROUPS

Groups are one of the two main powerhouses of Linkedin. It is within groups that you can begin the process of developing your voice and area of expertise. They also provide you with a place to network with others who have the same interests as you do, both personally and professionally. In fact, being part of a group will be one of the fastest ways to grow a network on Linkedin.

When you log in to Linkedin, you will be presented with a home page that lists the latest activity from people in your network. This includes their status updates, what they are reading, who they have connected with, whether they have updated their profile, who has recommended whom, AND, if you scroll down the page, you will see that there are various sections that gives you the **GROUP UPDATES** – this is how you can keep track of what's going on within the most active groups you are a member of.

There are two ways to find a group (or several) to join.

The first one is to click on the link that says Groups in the top menu that can be found on every page within Linkedin. The second is to type the following address directly into your browser address bar: http://www.Linkedin.com/groupsDirectory.

You can see the search menu on the right hand side of the main Groups page, (it is worth noting that the search menu now highlights groups in the drop down menu). Use keywords for your industry or company to find some listings for groups that may be appropriate for you. Remember, you may have to narrow your search down if you want to network only with people within your country or region. You can also click on Groups Directory and that will take you to a wider choice of search criteria.

It is worth noting that if you go straight to the Directory, you will be presented with a list of groups that are 'featured'. I can almost guarantee that you will not want (nor be able) to join most of these groups. Therefore you will need to use the search facility.

Once you have found a group you are interested in joining,  click on the "**Join Group**" link to request to join the group. Clicking the forward button lets you inform your connections that the group is available; this is useful if you know a number of them might not be aware that it exists, especially if they are interested in the same subject areas.

Groups are being created all the time and sometimes they are created for the wrong reasons. If you happen across one, you can use the 'Report as' link to highlight to Linkedin that you think there might be a problem. They can then investigate.

Remember though, your membership may be subject to review/approval by an administrator first. For instance, university and corporate groups may require a valid e-mail associated with the account. If you have any questions about joining a group, you can send a message to the group owner listed on the group information page.

MY GROUPS

Once you have joined a group you can find it again by clicking on My Groups, which appears in the drop down menu under the GROUPS tab. This will take you to YOUR specific group home page and will allow you to see at a glance the most recent activity on each.

You will also notice that underneath each Group are two drop down menus, the first is 'Go To' and the second is 'Actions'.

'Go To' takes you to the different sections of the group, for instance the Overview (home page) for the group, settings and member list.

'Actions' gives you the options to start a discussion; forward the group details to a contact or leave the group.

You can see some of the groups of which I am a member on the right hand side of the page. You will notice that they are not in alphabetical order – this is because I reordered them through my settings to display the ones I work with most frequently at the top.

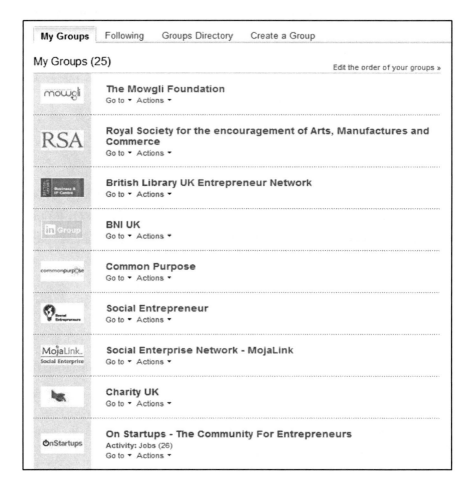

Your own homepage also gives you an overview of the most recent activity in the most active of the groups you belong to and allows you to take part in a private discussion. You can also click on the "Group Profile" link to view information about the group such as the owner, managers, website, and other information. When you go to a group, you have a number of things you can do and the menu bar will display these for you.

Mostly, it should be fairly self-explanatory. For instance, Discussions will take you to the list of discussions that are taking place with the most recent and/or popular at the top of the list. 'Members' takes you to the list of members and Search allows you to search the archive of the group.

The More tab though has a number of drop down options:

- Updates
- My Activity
- My Settings
- Sub Groups
- Group Profile

The most useful of these menu options is, in my opinion, the Updates.

GROUP UPDATES

Group Updates allows you to see the most recent activity in a specific group. The image below shows you the most recent activity from The Mowgli Foundation. You will see who has commented on different discussions and who has started a discussion and who has joined the group.

I can, if I choose, also enter the various discussions, engage and interact with my peers on the topics and subjects that I am most interested in and thereby demonstrate my knowledge, experience, skill or general wit and wisdom – depending on the mood I am in.

 Remember, getting involved in discussions is one of the fastest ways to ensure that you are seen as an expert.

GROUP DISCUSSIONS

Clicking on the name of a group will take you to a group home page. It is from here that you will be able to monitor almost all of the activity that is taking place, including the discussions that people are having. You can see that the most recent discussions are displayed on the left hand side of the home page of the Group you are viewing. On the right you will see the most recent activity of some of the people in the group.

You have the chance to get involved right at the top of the home page every time you log in and it's in this box that you can start a new discussion or add a link to an item of interest that you'd like other members of the group to see.

Immediately underneath this update box is a section that asks 'Would the group like these new discussions?'. This scrolls through the most recent activity automatically and it changes every three or four seconds.

On the right hand side of the screen you will see that there are updates  from other members of the group. Further down the page you will also find a small notification box that tells you who is the most influential person in the group – at that moment in time. Influence will be determined by things like the number of times they get involved in discussions or add a new item themselves. Unfortunately, at present it doesn't give statistics, but maybe that will be an update from the good people at Linkedin in the future.

DISCUSSIONS

The discussions tab takes you to a page which displays the most recent discussions for this group.

When you click on the title of a discussion, you will be taken to a new page which shows you who has asked the question, the question itself together with a little more preamble to expand it and then either a series of answers from people that have already taken part or a new comment box as in the image below.

It is in this comment box that you would write your own reply, which may be a suggestion, comment or an opinion. If you want to, you can also include links to external sites simply be typing in the whole web address including the http:// bit, for instance http://lindaph.me

If you want to be kept up to date with discussions perhaps because you asked the question or if it's a subject that's particularly relevant, then you can tick the *follow this discussion*' box that appears directly underneath your comment.

The purpose of a discussion is, naturally, to ask a question. This could be a leading question that is one you already know the answer to; it could be a piece of research or it could just be to start a debate. What is important though is that the question entices people to respond to you. The question at the beginning of the discussions section of the book was answered 316 times in the three months it had been active. It was also one of the most popular in this particular group (On-Startup if you are interested) which means that it will always appear in the home page of the group, until it is overtaken by another that is more popular.

Can you begin to understand that the person that asks a popular question is the person that is in front of all the group members that are active, regardless of the size of the group? This is the reason why Groups are one of the best and fastest ways to grow a network.

When you ask a question you can also add it as a piece of news, you do this by selecting the 'Attach a Link' underneath the discussion box. This provides you with the facility to add a link to a piece of news, useful resource or other website that you think your fellow members might be interested in. Once you have added the whole web address in the box, you simply click Attach and then Share and it will made available on the home page of the group immediately.

This can be a great way to build traffic to your website or blog – but only if it's highly appropriate to the general themes and discussions that take place. If it isn't, then you run the risk of the Administrators removing the news item and/or banning you for spamming the members.

JOBS

On the next page you will see the jobs board from the UK Charity group that I happen to be a member of. You can see that type of vacancy is highly variable, as are the salaries.

If you click on one of the links, you should be taken to some further details that should tell you how to apply – this isn't always the case as it will depend on the skill of the person posting the job advert, as to whether they remembered that people might like to know more about it.

Jobs: Recent Activity (11)

Project Manager - Somerset based
Posted 1 day ago by ███████ , HR recruiter I HR recruitment I writing CVs that work I photographer
Follow discussion | Add comment »

Head of Fundraising & Partnerships - Maternity Contract Part or Full Time Considered - Central London - £45,000 circa
Posted 3 days ago by ███████ , Director of Langton Not 4 Profit Ltd - Charity Recruitment Specialists
Follow discussion | Add comment »

Head of Supporter Relations - Christian Charity - Central London - £35,000 circa
Posted 3 days ago by ███████ , Director of Langton Not 4 Profit Ltd - Charity Recruitment Specialists
Follow discussion | Add comment »

Legacies Fundraiser - Healthcare Charity - Essex - £30,000 circa
Posted 3 days ago by ███████ , Director of Langton Not 4 Profit Ltd - Charity Recruitment Specialists
Follow discussion | Add comment »

Research Foundation Fundraiser - Association - Leicestershire - £27,000 - £37,000
Posted 3 days ago by ███████ , Director of Langton Not 4 Profit Ltd - Charity Recruitment Specialists
Follow discussion | Add comment »

HR Policy and Communications Consultant, Salary – From £29,244, Location – Flexible
Posted 9 days ago by ███████ , Recruitment and Retention Consultant at NSPCC
Follow discussion | Add comment »

Organisational Development Consultant – Safer Recruitment for Children, Salary – From £35,436, Location – Flexible
Posted 9 days ago by ███████ , Recruitment and Retention Consultant at NSPCC
Follow discussion | Add comment »

French speaking Senior Finance Officer - Grants Management @ International Alert - £34k. Know anyone for this role? Earn a £2k referral payment.
Posted 9 days ago by ███████ , New Business Manager - Charities at Mypeoplebiz.com
Follow discussion | Add comment »

International Alert: Great Lakes Regional Finance and Administration Manager - £38,928 per annum. Know anyone for this role? Earn a £2.3k referral payment.
Posted 9 days ago by ███████ , New Business Manager - Charities at Mypeoplebiz.com
Follow discussion | Add comment »

SUBGROUPS

Subgroups are a subset of existing groups and they allow those that come in different flavours to sub divide by country or even by region or speciality. Most groups will never need to use this facility, because they are contained by subject matter rather than by geographic location. Bear in mind that if you do decide to join a sub-group that you will automatically be given membership of (and access to) the parent group as well.

MEMBERS

Your group's Members page allows you to view all the members in your group. When you are a member of a group, you will always appear at the top of the list and then those you are connected to directly will appear below you. Underneath them will be the list of members you aren't directly connected to.

This is also one of the clearest ways to demonstrate the importance of your 'baby bio', the strapline that appears at the top of your profile page. This is because it is the item that will entice people in to read your profile.

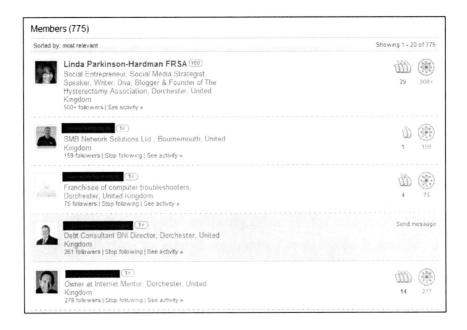

MY SETTINGS

This allows you to change all of the settings associated with your membership of any particular group, including how you wish to be kept updated about changes and activity. For instance, you may not wish to receive daily digests and you may prefer not to let people know that you are a member of a particular group, especially if you're job hunting.

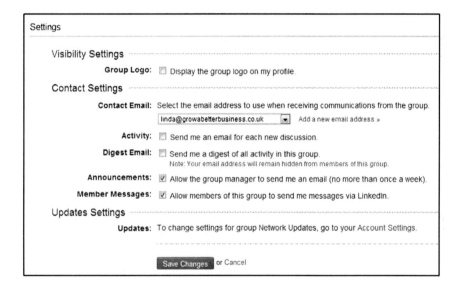

 Remember you can turn off the email digest simply by clicking on the settings for the groups of which you are a member.

EXERCISE

It is now time to find the groups that are most relevant for you to join, but before you do, you must think about why you are joining them.

Think about the overall objective for using Linkedin that you identified in the getting started chapter of this book; will the groups you are looking at help you to meet that objective? Finding the groups that will help you meet your objective is key, because you will be far more likely to engage with them on a regular basis if you do.

Use the **GROUPS DIRECTORY,** which you can find by clicking on the drop down menu under GROUPS in the top navigation bar, to find the groups that will best meet your needs by using keywords from your industry to identify them. The alternate way to find relevant groups is to have a look at the profiles of some of your contacts to see which groups they are members of.

Don't forget that groups can be based all over the world, and may not have professionals in this country as a member. You need to take a view on whether this is relevant or not. For instance, you could be the only professional based in the UK in the group and therefore gain an international reputation; or you might want to work within a specific legal framework that isn't appropriate or functional outside the country that you work/live in.

It might be helpful to pick **THREE** key areas that you think will help you meet the objective you have identified. For instance, my key areas might be web design, mentoring, social enterprise and writing and publishing.

I've made it possible to add three on the next page, you may have more or you may have just one; either way they will be a starting point to help you identify the most relevant groups.

For instance, I might be looking to grow the number of members for The Hysterectomy Association. As I already know that the target market (women having surgery) are unlikely to want their co-contacts to know they have medical problems, I would probably have little success in encouraging them to use a group created for them. However, as my objective for the business is to educate women about the choices they have, and at the same time ensure they find the association **BEFORE** they have the operation, then one way to use Linkedin might be to target professionals working in this field.

As one thing that **MUST** happen is that they are referred to a surgeon by their GP (in the UK at least), I could, therefore, use Linkedin groups to find medical professionals who are able, and willing, to help me get my message to the GP and/or surgeon.

1	
2	
3	

Try to join one or two at a time only, otherwise you won't have the time to really get to know them. A good tip is to use keywords within the search bar at the top of every page that are specific to your industry, for instance I might use medicine, medical, gynaecology, general practitioner etc. Remember you can use the drop down menu next to the search bar to select, People, Jobs, Companies, Answers, Inbox (your own inbox), Groups.

Make a note below of the other groups you found, but didn't join, as they could be useful in the future and you can go back and join them at a later date.

1	
2	
3	
4	
5	

SHOULD I START A GROUP?

Many people quite like the idea of starting their own group on Linkedin, they feel (quite rightly) that is a great way to gain exposure not only for themselves, but also for their skills and abilities, as well as their interests.

However, I would say that this needs to be treated with caution. Anyone can start a group, it is easy to do so, but it takes time, effort and organisation to maintain it, grow it and keep it vibrant.

I manage groups on Linkedin on behalf of clients and I need to access the group every day to monitor membership requests, moderate discussions that are being posted, start and encourage discussions, invite new members and generally nurture them into self-sustaining growth. It takes around twelve months of hard and daily work, to get a group to a level where it no longer needs a nursemaid.

If you don't have the time to devote to this activity, please reconsider starting a group and consider joining an appropriate one instead, it will be far more enjoyable.

CHAPTER 9 - ASKING AND ANSWERING QUESTIONS

I belong to fab local business network. We meet three times each month at different venues around Dorset for a breakfast session. At each meeting we are given the opportunity to explore our *'wicked issues'* (those things that are worrying us about our business) with a small group of people under the watchful eyes of a facilitator. I have lost count of the number of times someone has had a 'eureka' moment as a result of one of these sessions.

Not only are our wicked issues discussed in the groups, but an email is also generated by the organiser very shortly afterwards. This email is sent out to **ALL** the members of the network and contains the wicked issues each member attending discussed.

This means is that the power of the WHOLE group can be brought to bear, because as members, we are encouraged to get in touch if we think we have an answer to the question.

Linkedin Answers serves a very similar function, without the full English breakfast, and is one of the very best ways on the web to:

- Ask a question and get fast, accurate answers from your network and other experts worldwide
- Showcase your knowledge, expertise, and interests by answering questions

- Keep up with the latest news in your industry and/or functional area

You can find the Answers section by clicking on MORE tab in the top navigation bar and then selecting Answers from the drop down menu provided.

ANSWERING QUESTIONS

You can showcase your knowledge and interests by answering questions. The answers you provide become part of your public profile which can be seen on the right hand side of the View My Profile tab in Profile. (This is what people visiting your profile will see.)

If they click on 'See all Q&A', they are presented with your most recent questions

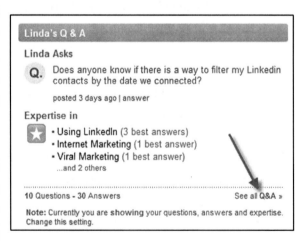

and your 30 most recent answers. It is in this area that you then get the opportunity to demonstrate your expertise to connections, potential business partners or employers.

Questions (and Answers) can be found quickly in these places:

- When a connection asks a question, you'll receive an update on your home page when you next log in to Linkedin
- As an email if the person asking has chosen to send it directly to you
- Under the Answers tab, where you can find links to:
    - Advanced Answers Tab
    - My Q&A
    - Ask A Question
    - Answer A Question

Clicking on a question will bring up a new page with the question and any answers that have already been submitted. It is important to remember that most questions are only open for a period of seven days (unlike discussions which remain open permanently).

When you **answer** a question, your answers will appear:

- Under the question you answered
- As a network update on the homepages of your connections
- On your profile in the Q&A box in the right hand column
- In an email to the person who asked the question.
- As part of that little activity link on your 'baby bio' that pops up in all sorts of places around Linkedin.

You can also answer a question privately. If you do, your answer never appears

anywhere on the site, instead it is sent by email to the person who asked the question.

HOW CAN I EARN EXPERTISE?

According to Linkedin; *"Expertise is a feedback measure from your fellow users. Every time the questioner picks your answer as the best, you gain a point of expertise in the category of the question. The best way you can gain expertise is to answer questions in the areas you know. Experts in each area are recognized on Linkedin: the more points of expertise you gain, the higher you appear on lists of experts."*

If you want to jump right in to answering questions then you can find them under the subject areas that are listed on the right hand side of the Answers home page. You can also find the most recent questions posed right on that same home page. You will also find questions that people you are connected to have already answered on your own home page too.

HOW DO I ASK A QUESTION?

There are three different ways you can ask a question:

1. When you go to Answers the first thing you will see is a big orange box (it's orange so that it's really noticeable) that says **"Ask a Question"** and **"Answer a Question"**.
2. There is also a text link on the right hand side of the same screen that says **"Ask a question now"** – you can see it under the My Q&A heading.

3. Finally, you could use the tab on the Answers home page that is titled **Ask A Question**

However you start to ask a question, you will find yourself at the following page on Linkedin.

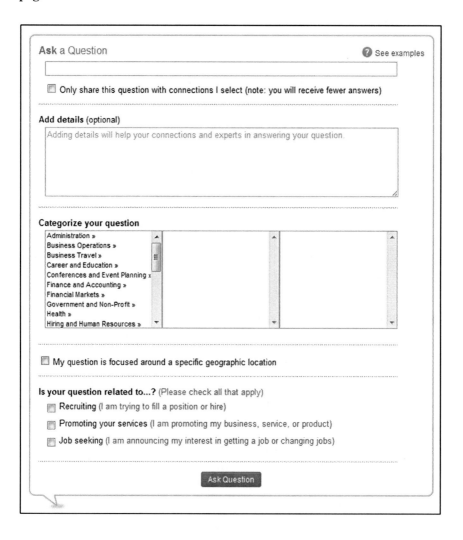

When you ask a question it will immediately appear in the following places:

- Under the Answers tab
- On your profile page
- on the Linkedin homepage of your connections
- In an email, if you sent your question to any specific connections

You can also ask your question privately. If you choose to do so, your question will not appear on the site, and is instead delivered as a message to the specific connections you chose.

 Remember, if you want your question to go to the whole of your network rather than selected individuals, you must use the SKIP THIS link provided at the bottom of the page that asks you to add contacts.

ADVANCED QUESTION TECHNIQUES

You can also find out if your question has already been answered by doing a keyword search on the Advanced Answers Search tab. You can then find out if others have asked a similar question in the past. Read through the answers to see if they meet your needs. If they don't then go ahead and ask the question again or consider rephrasing it to be more specific.

Exercises

1. Now is the time to **ANSWER** a question that someone has already posed in your network. Make sure it is something you feel

happy to respond to and that it allows you to demonstrate some knowledge you have already.

2. Next, try asking a **QUESTION** and send it out either to your network, your group contacts or the Linkedin community. For instance, what is your 'Wicked Issue' of the moment?

CHAPTER 10 - PROMOTING YOUR LINKEDIN PROFILE

Promoting your Linkedin profile can be as simple as creating a Linkedin button for your website or blog and adding the web address for your profile to your email signature.

Alternatively, you can make it a whole lot more complex by doing such things as:

- adding your Linkedin profile address (or button) to any other profiles on social networks/social media you belong to
- add it to your signature on any forums or other discussion groups you happen to belong to, particularly if they have a professional element to them at all
- make sure that your profile settings are set to show your 'Full Profile' as this is indexed by the search engines
- invite more people to join you, as you do so, they'll get to know about your Linkedin activity too
- become active on groups and answer questions especially as these are indexed by the search engines too
- add it to your CV, portfolio and/or promotional literature and stationary
- add it to your business card

- add it to any presentations and proposals you put together – particularly if you have relevant recommendations and/or experience listed on your profile

- don't forget to create a personalised URL for your profile; mine is **www.Linkedin.com/in/lindaph** - instructions are given below.

CREATING A LINKEDIN BUTTON FOR YOUR BLOG OR WEBSITE

1. Click the Profile link in the top navigation bar of the website and choose the Edit My Profile tab and click on Edit Public Profile Settings.

2. Click on the **Customised Buttons** Link below the URL.

3. This shows you a variety of buttons and the code next to them, when you have chosen the one you want simply click **ONCE** in the box with the code next to the image you want, then click **CTRL** and **C** on your keyboard, this will copy the code for you.

4. Next login to the dashboard of your blog or website and add it to the page, sidebar or text widget by 'pasting' it in its entirety according to whichever element your particular system happens to use.

CHAPTER 11 - LINKEDIN APPLICATIONS

If Linkedin is the place to showcase your professional career, business, skills and expertise, it would make sense for it to provide a number of different ways that allow you to showcase a number of different aspects to your working life.

They could have chosen the route of creating a number of systems that allow you to write articles, show presentations and have meetings. Instead though, they have chosen some essential elements (such as creating and promoting events) to manage themselves and then create links and connections with other online systems that are far better at providing specific services than they could ever be. This is a great example of only doing what you are good at, and not trying to be all things to all men.

Welcome to the Linkedin Applications directory, a repository of very useful applications that allow you to extend your profile beyond the confines of the Linkedin software to the wider world around it. This is actually a very clever marketing ploy as well, as it means that people are more likely to stay within Linkedin, rather than go off to one of the other networks around.

The purpose of Linkedin Applications is to expand the usefulness of the network to its users. There are sixteen at the time of writing and I am certain that more will be added in the months to come.

So, what sort of activities do they allow you to do?

- You can share with your network the books you are reading and those you want to read, as well as what you think of them. It's a great way to share knowledge and expertise

- Add articles and blog posts you have written to your profile automatically. Viewers can pick up your articles and learn more about your business

- Find out if there is anyone making the same trip as you so you can catch up with them for a meeting.

- Show videos and presentations you've created or used to a brand new audience.

- Monitor what's being said about your business or company on twitter.

- Let people know about the events you are running and attending.

Linkedin Applications work in a variety of different ways. In some instances they gather the most recent updates to the account you have specified (twitter is a great example of this). For instance, I have added the various different blogs I write on to my profile. The THREE most recent posts I have written will now display on my profile page, as well as on my home page.

In other applications you simply create the content right there in Linkedin and Linkedin 'events' is a good example of this in action. And in still others, you might interact with the application in Linkedin, but the information and content you have created stays on the external system. Slideshare (the presentation software) is an excellent demonstration of this in action.

To add an application to your profile is reasonably simple. Just go to the applications page (you can find it in the Applications Directory, which is under the MORE tab in the top navigation bar) and click on the large icon for the one you want to use – BE WARNED: the order they are shown keeps changing, so you can never be sure which one is where on the page!

You will then be taken to a page on Linkedin that looks a little like the one above. On the left hand side, you will see some blurb about what the application is and on the right a box that asks you if you want to display the results of the application on your profile and on your home page.

If you want to add the application, and you already have an account, all you need to do is decide whether you want your Linkedin contacts to be able to see things on your profile and whether you want them to display on the home page so that you are prompted if something comes up that's interesting. Then click 'Add Application'.

Most of the time in order to activate these accounts, you will need at least one of the following pieces of information to connect to the application:

1. a username and/or password, or a keyword or two such as your business name
2. an RSS feed from your blog.

A Word about RSS Feeds

You can find the **RSS feed** (a special web address which lists all the most recent content) by looking for one of the following on your account page for the application you would like to include: RSS, ATOM or a image of a feed which looks like the one on the left. For instance, if I were to include the RSS feed from my slideshare account, I would log in to Slideshare and then find the link to the RSS feed. The icon for RSS looks something like the one to the left, but they may vary in colour and shape.

In the next few pages I'm going to give you an overview of some of the best (in my opinion) applications to use, particularly those that can be especially helpful in building your personal brand and helping you to connect with the people you want to work with.

SLIDESHARE

Slideshare is a fantastic way to make the content you create available to a wider audience. I use it to showcase presentations and documents that I'm happy for people to download, embed on websites or use because they promote me at the same time. In fact, sometimes slideshare is the best place to put this sort of material because it has a huge audience looking for it.

On my slideshare account, I have a number of presentations and documents about social media. You can find my account at *http://www.slideshare.net/lindaph1*.

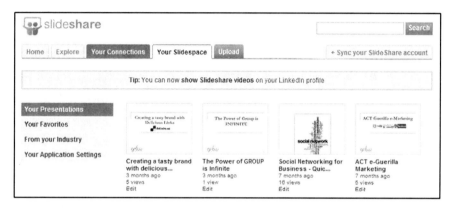

The Slideshare application on Linkedin allows you to embed your latest presentations automatically in your profile. It's an excellent way to showcase training materials and business presentations. When you (or someone viewing your profile) clicks on the **View All Your Presentations** link, it takes you to all the presentations you have loaded into slideshare even though you are within Linkedin. What's more, you can even upload new presentations to slideshare from within Linkedin and you don't even have to go to your account on slideshare.

Bear in mind though, that the number of views you get on Linkedin is going to be VERY different from the number you get on Slideshare itself. For instance, the presentations and documents shown above have the following differences:

	Slideshare Views	Linkedin Views
Creating a tasty brand with delicious links	1219	6
The Power of GROUP is Infinite	1033	1
Social Networking for Business	9592	16
Act e-Guerrilla Marketing	1928	5

Just a small discrepancy! However, this doesn't mean that embedding the presentations in your profile it a bad thing this is because for it to count as a 'view' it needs to be clicked on from within your profile, therefore the number of people that see it on your profile aren't included in the numbers shown.

READING LIST BY AMAZON

The Reading List by Amazon application is a handy little networking tool more which allows you to see who else is interested in the same books (subjects) that you are interested in. It also allows you to share with your peers the sorts of books you think that they might like too.

If there is someone in your network that you think is particularly good at what they do, then watching their reading list might be a way to emulate them, or acquire the knowledge that they have.

Finally, you can find out which books are the ones that are 'hot' in your industry by clicking on the 'Industry Updates' tab. This is an excellent way to identify changing trends.

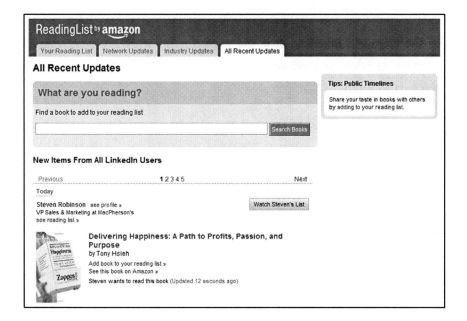

LINKEDIN POLLS

A Linkedin Poll is simply a statement or question that can have up to five responses.

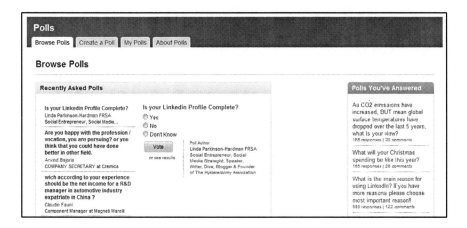

This is one of the few applications in the directory that have been created by the team at Linkedin. It is the perfect solution if you want a quick overview of what your connections feel about a specific topic or question you have in mind.

I will sometimes use it to find out the current *state of the nation* for a particular subject I'm interested in or to learn about current trends in a given area, mostly through finding polls that have been answered as I don't often use it to create my own.

To use it you simply click on Create a Poll in the application tab, type your question, give up to five possible responses which can be rotated randomly and then decide if you want to pay to get responses from the United States or your own network (the latter is free by the way – the former you will have to pay for). Then press next and your poll is created! It is now viewable on your profile, your home page and on your contacts home page too.

COMPANY BUZZ

By now, I would imagine that everyone using Linkedin has at least heard of Twitter, even if they don't have an account on the network.

The Company Buzz application is another of the applications created by Linkedin, the difference with this one though is that it pulls in any information about your business whenever it is mentioned *BY NAME* on twitter. It's a great way to keep up to date with what people are saying about you. For instance, I keep an eye on the buzz around my own businesses, as well as those of the clients whose social media account I happen to manage.

The image overleaf shows you the results for The Hysterectomy Association. You can see that they are all about a single topic, 'The Complete Guide to Hysterectomy and Beyond', which is a complete set of all the books, booklet and guides that we produce in eBook form.

You could also use this application to track search terms if you wanted to as well, but it's often easier to do that in one of the many twitter clients that you can find online.

When you first activate the application it will check your profile and look for any organisations or businesses you have listed on your profile. You can then edit them to remove them if you wish. For instance I had links to The National Trust and Manchester University, simply because they were on my profile.

You can also create a new search term as well by using the search box that you saw on the screen shot. When the search has been run, you will be given the opportunity to save it.

EVENTS

The events application from the Linkedin team is one of the most popular applications on the network and almost everyone I know is using it. It gives you the opportunity to find events that your connections are either attending or organising and it also allows you to list your own events and then tell your contacts about them.

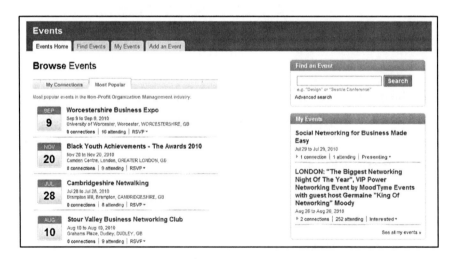

In many cases the events will also have a website that you can visit to make a booking.

GOOGLE PRESENTATION

The Google Presentation application is very similar in function to Slideshare, it allows you to upload presentations, videos and documents and then display them directly in your profile. It is also the only way I know of to show a video on your profile, which would be ideal for online trainers who are regularly creating 'how to' guides.

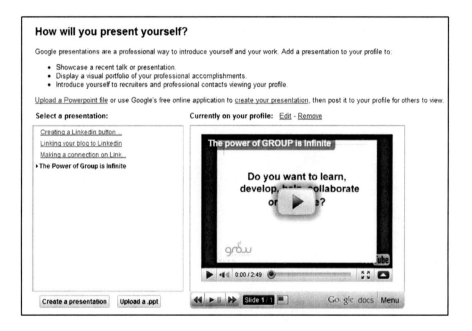

You will notice in the image on the left that I have two areas to work with. The left hand side shows the presentations I have added to Google and the one on the right shows the presentation that is currently on my profile. To change the presentation on your profile, you simply need to select it from the list and save it.

Unfortunately, if you want to add a video to your presentation you can't upload them from within Linkedin as you can with Slideshare. You will need to create the document in Google and then select it from the list.

TWEETS

This is the twitter application that works within your profile and unlike Company Buzz it is looking for YOUR twitter account and those of the people you are following on twitter.

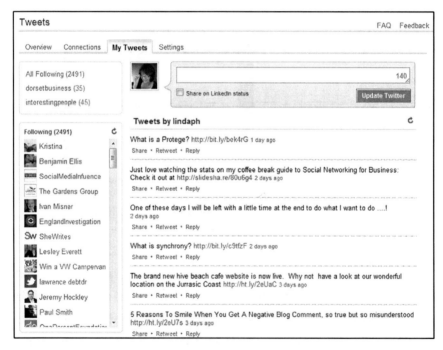

If you have more than one twitter account listed on your profile (as I do) then it will select the primary account to work with directly.

This is also the application that allows you to post out your Linkedin status updates to your twitter account/s from your home page.

You will see in the image overleaf that I have the option to see My Tweets or those of the people I follow on Twitter. The top box on the left hand side shows the two lists I have created on twitter as well; clicking on those would bring up only tweets from those people I have added to the lists.

If I click on Connections, I will see tweets from my Linkedin connections and I can then choose to follow them or not on twitter right from within Linkedin.

The application also gives me the opportunity to drill down to an individual's twitter account so I can see what they've been up to most recently, again all without leaving the comfort of Linkedin.

WORDPRESS

Wordpress, for those who aren't familiar with it, is my favourite blogging tool. It gives millions the opportunity to present their thoughts and opinions on almost any topic to the world, in a very simple and easy to use system. If you fancy having a go at blogging, just head on over to those nice people at www.wordpress.com and grab an account.

This particular application relies on picking up the RSS Feed from a specific account and it will then display the most recent five posts that you have written in your profile and/or home page should you wish it to.

An RSS Feed address from wordpress.com for those who aren't familiar with them will look something like:

http://YOURWORDPRESSACCOUNT.wordpress.com/feed/ and you can choose to show ALL your recent posts or only those tagged 'Linkedin'.

TRIPIT

Tripit is the travel companion application that allows you to find out whether anyone you know is travelling to your part of the world or if they will also be in the vicinity of a meeting you may be having away from home.

From the home page of the application, you will see your own trips plus anyone from your network who is going to be close to you at the same time. However, the power of this application is in the number of people that use it. If your contacts aren't using it, then you won't see where they are and won't be able to suggest meeting up.

COMPANIES

When you click on the More tab, one of the items in the drop down menu is Companies. If

- Social Media Strategist at The Mowgli Foundation ☐
- Director at Grow A Better Business ☐ (Sole Proprietorship)
- CEO at The Hysterectomy Association ☐ (Sole Proprietorship)

you then view one of your contacts, you may well find that their profile has a little symbol next to their current and past companies that looks a little like a sheet of paper. This indicates that this company has created a *business profile* on Linkedin. However, don't get too excited; Linkedin is primarily focused on individuals and the Company profile is a limited application that allows a business to share standard information across all of its current and past employees.

Following one of the links that these pages contain takes you to a page that gives you an overview of the company, together with a list of its current and past employees as well as the activity that has recently been undertaken at the company. Activity includes things like new people joining, changes to other peoples profiles and recent departures.

If your company or business doesn't yet have a profile listed, it is easy to add one by clicking on the **Add Company** link that you will find from any company profile you read.

This will take you to a simple form that contains standard information such as year the company was founded, number of employees, an overview and contact details. Bear in mind though, if you are an employee of a large company then you might not be the right person to create this profile and you will need to talk to the marketing or HR departments to see if there is someone more appropriate to undertake the task.

CHAPTER 12 – LINKEDIN RECIPES FOR SUCCESS

In the coming pages I want to share with you a some specific 'recipes' that you can follow to help you be more effective at a wide range of activities that can help you in your business or in your career (and sometimes in both).

The map on the next page how the recipes have been organised. To use them, choose the topic that most interests you and then choose one of the strategies listed to work with first. You may want (or need) to do more than one to achieve the goal you have in mind, but it is important to focus on just one to start with

You can find more '**recipes for successes**' at my personal blog: www.womanontheedgeofreality.com

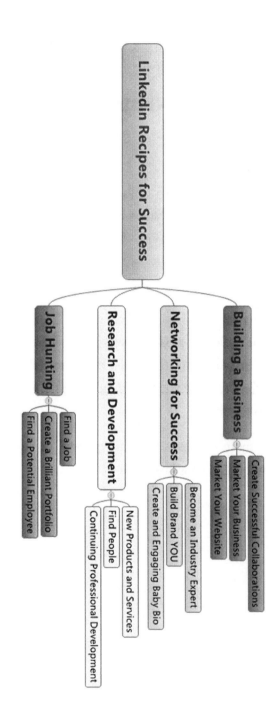

BUILDING A BUSINESS

There are many different actions and activities required to build a business. This set of three recipes will concentrate on:

1. Creating a Successful Collaboration
2. Marketing your Business
3. Marketing your Website

Each of these activities is designed to ensure that you, and your business, are in front of the right people at the right time.

CREATE A SUCCESSFUL COLLABORATION

According to dictionaries, to collaborate in this sense means to work jointly with others or to cooperate with an agency or organisation to which you may not be directly connected. In other words, this is working towards a partnership to achieve a single goal or aim, perhaps the delivery of a particular product or service to a specific client. An example of successful collaborations might be the author who works with an illustrator; or the website developer who works with a graphic designer, photographer and a copywriter. None of these are permanent business relationships; they are simply formed to deliver a specific project.

The activities that one would need to undertake to create a successful collaboration are:

- Find people with whom one shares similar values and ethics
- Ensure that those people have the skills needed to complete the work
- Check the quality of work undertaken and their ability to deliver on time and to budget

Therefore the actions one needs to take on Linkedin are:

1. Create a project brief that is as specific as you are able to make it. This should include requirements, skills set, time scales, location and any other pertinent information
2. Undertake a search for individuals or companies within your network who have the required skill set. This may mean searching by keyword for specific terminology

3. Ask for suggestions of suitable suppliers from your network by posting a status update, sending a direct request or by asking a question

4. When you have a list of possible candidates, read their profiles and check any links they may have provided to their business websites, portfolios or other online materials

5. Find out about employee skills, knowledge and understanding

6. Read any testimonials and check their activity in any groups you have access to

7. Create a shortlist of possible candidates and then contact them individually to find out if they are interested in the type of work of you are proposing and are able to deliver within the time frame you specify

8. Ask them to send in a formal written proposal.

MARKET YOUR BUSINESS

As I was often told, the world is full of amazing products that are gathering dust simply for lack of a sale. Without marketing, no one will know that either you, or your business exist. As much effort needs to be put into creating a marketing strategy as is put into product and service development and delivery.

The activities you need to engage in to market your business include:

- Understand who your target market is and why they might want to buy what you are selling
- Decide which of the various groups you could sell to are the priority
- Determine the most appropriate 'key message' that they are likely to respond to.

To market your business on Linkedin, you will need to:

1. Create a business profile through the Companies application
2. Add your 'Follow Us on Linkedin' badge to your company website
3. Update your personal profile to include details of specialities and the goals that you have set for the company
4. Regularly answer questions that are posted about your market sector
5. Talk about what your business is doing in your status updates
6. If you are hosting any events, don't forget to include them in Linkedin Events and invite your network contacts
7. Create a slideshare and/or Google Presentations account. Upload company presentations and share them on your profile

8. Import your company (or personal if appropriate) blog into your personal profile and your Company profile

9. Add the company Twitter account to your Linkedin profile to ensure that any status updates you add are broadcast to your Twitter followers

10. Join in discussions in relevant industry groups

11. Consider using Linkedin Adverts to promote specific skills, products or services

12. Ask for recommendations from clients that you know are happy and satisfied with the work you have done on their behalf

13. Stay in contact with connections and keep them informed about developments in your business.

MARKET YOUR WEBSITE

A website needs exposure as much as a business does in order to encourage people to come and have a look at what you are doing, the products and services you offer and to find out what distinguishes your business from your competitors. There is much you can do to help yourself, but essentially, the tasks you will need to undertake are:

- Be visible online. This includes adding your link to relevant directories, lists and industry specific websites
- Ensure that you are adding interesting information to your website on a regular basis as this will encourage visitors to come and read what you have to say
- Make sure that your website has a mechanism that captures information from those people who are interested in what you have to offer. This might be a subscription option or a simple form that allows people to get a brochure delivered.

On Linkedin the tasks that will be most effective in marketing your website are those that will generate interest in what you have to say and you should consider becoming active in at least some of the following areas:

1. Update your personal profile, and encourage other staff members to update theirs, to include links to your company website and/or blog

2. Whenever you answer a question don't forget to include a link to your company website in the 'web resources' section of the answer form

3. Regularly post links to interesting material in your status update

4. Import your company (or personal if appropriate) blog into your personal profile and your Company profile

5. Add the company Twitter account to your Linkedin profile to ensure that any status updates with website links in are broadcast to your Twitter followers

6. Add a news item to your groups whenever you create a new article to your website.

NETWORKING FOR SUCCESS

It is unlikely that you would be active on Linkedin if you weren't aware about how powerful networking can be. However, that said, there is an art to networking that creates the difference between being a successful networker and a mediocre networker. Typically this is demonstrated by successful networkers who know that the person they are 'talking' to, whether that is online or in the physical world, are usually not the people they are selling to. The purpose of networking is to build a relationship that is formed out of trust. That trust will allow the people you have relationships with to recommend you to their friends, colleagues and clients safe in the knowledge that you will deliver on the promises you make.

In this section, you will find three recipes to help you:

- Be recognised as an industry expert
- Build your personal brand
- Create an engaging baby-bio

BECOME AN INDUSTRY EXPERT

What exactly is an Industry expert? To my mind these are the people to whom I would go if I had a question that I couldn't answer, because I know that they have more experience than I do. Even if they can't answer the question directly, they will almost certainly know where to look for the answer. They are usually people who like to help others and who aren't worried about keeping the knowledge they have secret.

There are three ways to become an industry expert:

- To write about what you know in journals, magazines and periodicals
- To make presentations to groups about the market sector you work in
- To answer peoples questions in public

Linkedin allows you to do all of these activities in a highly public way and the actions you need to take are:

1. Develop your profile to demonstrate and qualify why you are able to talk with authority about the subjects you are interested in
2. Take part in discussions in relevant groups and where appropriate share links to things you have written to back up the opinion you are sharing
3. Answer questions that other people have posed about the subjects you are knowledgeable about
4. Import your blog into your Linkedin profile so that contacts can see what you are writing about

108

5. Add links to articles you have published or books you have written as news items in your groups

6. Use status updates to post links to all your contacts that allow them to read what you have written online

7. Ask for, and accept, recommendations from contacts you have worked with. You may also wish to ask for them in a specific format

8. Include speaking engagements, presentations you are making and events you are taking part in, in the events section of Linkedin

9. Use Amazon Reading List to share with your contacts the books that you have found helpful.

BUILD BRAND 'YOU'

Personal branding is all the rage now and it involves creating an image of you that is both appropriate and sustainable. It works on the premise that we will all have many different roles over the course of a lifetime and that each one of those roles informs the person we are at the present time. This work involves ensuring that our public persona is the one that we wish to promote at any time and requires the following actions to be undertaken on a regular basis:

- Having an up to date profile
- Consistently developing a network of people that know who you are and what you do
- Be visible within that network and to the people you want to get to know

Linkedin is the perfect place to begin building a Personal Brand and the activities that will be most helpful include:-

1. Ensuring that your profile is filled out completely, this includes past positions as well as your education and a photograph
2. Keeping your profile updated with any changes, this includes contact details
3. Creating a custom URL that you can use on a business card, email signature or in other promotional literature
4. Writing an eye-catching baby-bio that encourages people to take a deeper look at who you are

5. Regularly adding connections to your Linkedin profile, particularly those people you have met and who are influential within your industry

6. Use the specialities and summary section of your profile to add in specific keywords for the work you do

7. Consider importing your contacts and connecting with as many as possible

8. Aim to get in touch with at least one person every day even if it's just to say hello

9. Include all your contact details in your profile, especially your email address

10. Change your settings to show the maximum visible profile to the search engines

11. If you are attending an event make sure you list you are attending through Linkedin Events.

CREATE AN ENGAGING BABY-BIO

An interesting and engaging baby-bio is what helps people to decide whether or not they are going to read more about you when they find you through a Linkedin Search, Group member list or Answer.

Your baby bio, needs to summarise in one line who you are, what you do and what makes you stand out from the crowd. My current baby-bio reads "*Social Entrepreneur, Social Media Strategist, Speaker, Writer, Diva, Blogger & Founder of The Hysterectomy Association*". It says exactly what I do and gives me a way of asserting authority about the things I talk about on Linkedin. In fact, I use the same baby-bio in many different places online.

If you want to be seen by the people that matter on Linkedin then the actions you need to take are:

1. Your headline (baby bio) will be set automatically to the job you listed as your current or most recent, this needs to be changed
2. Search for and read the baby bio of other people in your industry on Linkedin
3. Ask your clients what makes you different from your competitors
4. Check out the people who are active in Answers
5. Include your specialities or location (if this is important)
6. Use the search facility to find the people who are most connected within your industry to see what they have included in their baby bio

7. Don't forget to include a photograph as this is often shown in conjunction with your baby bio and plays a key part in whether people remember meeting you or not.

RESEARCH AND DEVELOPMENT

All businesses, whatever their size and nature, are built upon the products and/or services that they sell to their customers and clients. It is also true to say that products come and go and services change according to politics, fashion and the media. Who, for instance, could have predicted the massive impact on every aspect of our lives that the Internet or mobile phones would have back in the 1980's.

In order to keep up with the pace of change we need to undertake a huge amount of research and development, not only about products and services, but also skill sets as new jobs come into being to reflect the change that happens.

In this section, you will find three recipes to help you:

- Research new products and services
- Find the right people for your job
- Ensure your knowledge and understanding reflects the latest trends and changes

RESEARCH PRODUCTS AND SERVICES

Having products to sell and services to offer are the lifeblood of any business, without these core components you don't actually have a business. And yet, these can change according to the season, global events and developments in technology. Now that we all have digital cameras there is no need for the photographic print shop who used to take a roll of film and provide us with a neat envelope containing 24 or 36 fixed size photographs to show to friends and relatives. All of a sudden we were able to take the photograph and print it ourselves. This change in technology meant that the industry had to adapt quickly or lose out altogether. We are also bombarded daily with information, data and reports; it seems we can hardly move for the avalanche of email that lands in our inbox. So how do you balance the need to know what is going on in your industry with the need to do the work?

Linkedin allows you to keep up to date with your market sector quickly and easily and to do so you will need to take the following actions:

1. Join relevant industry groups and take part in discussions
2. Make sure your group settings are set to receive Group Updates as a daily or weekly digest
3. Seek out key players on Linkedin and bookmark their profiles through your browser
4. Visit Linkedin Events regularly to find out what is happening in your industry
5. Follow relevant questions that are being asked in Linkedin Answers

6. Use a 'feed reader' to subscribe to the RSS feed for the Answers section you are interested in
7. Keep up to date with the latest industry books by using Amazon Reading List to find out what your industry is particularly interested in
8. Read the most recent and relevant presentations from those who are important in your market sector by finding them on their profile
9. Use the Polls feature to create quick overviews of an issue and ask your contacts to contribute
10. Find relevant industry blogs that are updated regularly by scanning your contacts profiles.

FIND PEOPLE

Most businesses would list their people as their most valuable asset and it goes without saying that for this to be the case, they need people who have the right combination of skill, attitude and knowledge in order to be successful.

Yet, recruitment is an area that is often fraught with complications and potential problems. To ensure you have the right people in the right place at the right time a business would normally need to undertake the following activities:

- Advertise a job as being available
- Accept and vet applications
- Interview and appoint the right client

Although Linkedin can do many things, one thing it can't do is the actual interview of a client. But it can do a lot to help ensure you are talking to the right people in the first place. In order to do that you will need to do the following actions:

1. Investigate the current role descriptions being used for a particular position by finding similar jobs through the job search function of the site
2. Post your job in the jobs section of Linkedin (this does have a cost attached to it)
3. Add your job to the jobs section of any relevant industry groups you are a member of

4. Contact your network to see if they have any recommendations of people who might be appropriate

5. Consider doing a search for current industry professionals who have the right skill set and make them a direct approach

6. After someone applies use Linkedin to check their profile and perhaps check their reference information

7. Use Linkedin as a resource to target the right questions to your candidates at interview. You could ask them about their current or past roles or what they think of a subject you know they have answered a question on

8. Looking up their contacts will give you a good idea of their network and how active they are in a specific market sector

CONTINUING PROFESSIONAL DEVELOPMENT

Undertaking continuing professional development (CPD) is often a requirement of on-going membership of a professional body and in many cases it usually involves attendance at key events, training courses and the successful completion of exams. Increasingly though, the professional bodies are also taking into account online activity as a sign of continuing competency to practice, at least for a part of the CPD requirement.

There are a number of ways in which Linkedin can help you keep your knowledge and understanding up to date and they include:

1. Being an active part of the Linked in community
2. Contributing to discussions in the Groups you belong to
3. Asking questions in Linkedin Answers
4. Taking part in conferences, training and webinars that are posted in Linkedin Events
5. Join groups for your professional body
6. Join the groups that have been set up for your University or College, especially if there are industry sub groups attached to them
7. Use the groups facility to find people you can add to your contact list
8. Use the filter facility in your Contact organiser to keep up to date with specific groups of people from the same industry.
9. Work your way through your contact list and add tags to each member so that you can find specific sets of skills and interests at a later date

10. Find out if people are visiting your area or attending the same events before you travel through the My Travel application.

JOB HUNTING

The focus of this book has been on supporting the business use of Linkedin and yet, there are more people using Linkedin who are employed than are running their own company. Many of the former group of people will change their job, their role even their whole career several times in the course of a lifetime.

This group of recipes is for the person who is looking for new job or careert and will cover the following three areas:

- Finding a job
- Creating an effective portfolio
- Finding a potential employer

FIND A JOB

Let's say you are an accountant and your partner has been offered a job in another part of the country. What will you do to accommodate their career development? Will you move with them and if so, will you be looking for another position as an accountant or even take the opportunity to go in a completely different direction.

Finding a new job is quite a daunting prospect for many people. In much the same way that employers have to take new recruits on blind faith that their resume and interview have given them the tools to be certain they will fit in; new employees will hope that the post they have just accepted will give them the opportunity to develop their career further in an environment that is both supportive and challenging.

So how can Linkedin ensure that you find the perfect new position, well if you do undertake the following activities, you will at least put yourself in a good starting place:

1. Ensure your profile is complete and up to date with details of your current role, specific responsibilities and goals.
2. Don't forget to list any achievements to date, especially those that can demonstrate you are able to deliver on targets
3. Join relevant industry groups and monitor the job board within them to see if anything appropriate is announced
4. Use the advanced job search to find posts in specific locations, levels and industries
5. Make a list of the current keywords that might be used to define the role you are looking for. For example, SEO and search engine

optimisation mean the same thing. You will minimise the potential for missing great jobs simply because you are looking for different terminology

6. Once you have found a possible job, research the company through the Company profile

7. Find out if there is anyone you are connected to that is employed by the same company. They may be able to fill you in on company details

8. Make sure that you have a great covering letter ready in a text file so that you can simply copy and paste it into this section of the Apply form

9. Don't forget to address it personally to the person who posted the job advert.

CREATE A BRILLIANT PORTFOLIO

For portfolio, read resume, CV or profile; one or more of these will be needed to apply for any position that is advertised, wherever that may be. This is the one piece of information that a future employer will judge you most harshly on and it needs to be the right information, presented in the best way to illustrate your suitability for the role you are applying for.

Your portfolio will also be used to help demonstrate three things:

- That your skill set and levels of experience are appropriate
- That you have experience
- You are the type of person who will fit into an existing team.

Linkedin will help you to do all of these activities and more if you use it to its fullest potential with the following actions:

1. I can't stress it highly enough, ensure your profile is up to date, accurate and complete. Add a current photograph too.
2. Create an engaging and interesting baby bio for your headline to help demonstrate that you understand the needs of the industry you are working in
3. Consider adding links to any personal websites or blogs, especially if they are relevant to your area of expertise
4. If you are able to, use the Slideshare or Google presentations applications to showcase presentations you have given (but consider copyright issues and check with your current employer before uploading if you created them on their behalf)

5. Respond to questions in the Answers section of Linkedin to demonstrate industry knowledge and understanding
6. Be active in groups, especially those that contain key players in the companies you might like to work with.

FIND A NEW EMPLOYER

Although this is similar, it's not quite the same as finding a job. This requires a different tactic and outside of Linkedin, would probably be undertaken by sending speculative letters and emails to potential employers to find out if there were any opportunities available.

However, within Linkedin we can employ some slightly different tactics that may have a greater chance of success in the longer term, although this can be a long game so be prepared to work at it for some time before getting a result.

The actions that could be successful include:

1. Find out which companies use the skills you offer and then filter them to find the ones that are right for you. This might be based on location, size, market sector or profile
2. Research the employee list through the Company application to find out whether there are any particular considerations around company values, ethics and culture
3. Using the employee list find out if there is anyone that you are connected to directly and get in touch to find out if they can point you to the right person to talk to
4. Ask your network of contacts if anyone can introduce you to the company, especially one or more of the people who might be responsible for recruitment to your particular area of interest
5. Once you have found the right person to contact, try to join the same groups, participate in the same discussions and answer the questions they have either asked or answered

6. Ask a question yourself and if someone at the company responds, ask them to connect with you, they can only say 'no'.

USEFUL RESOURCES

There are many resources that you might find useful that will help you use Linkedin even more effectively, and I have listed just a few of the ones I can be sure won't change to help you.

Linkedin Customer Support Centre

This has to be the first port of call if you have a question that doesn't seem to be answered anywhere else. You can find it at:
http://Linkedin.custhelp.com

Linkedin Learning Centre

This is the place to look for tutorials and short videos that show you what to do and how to do it. You can find it at: http://learn.Linkedin.com.

Linkedin Blog

The Linkedin Blog will keep you up to date with the latest news and updates on the network, it's at: http://blog.Linkedin.com/

Official Linkedin YouTube Channel

There are a huge number of videos that walk you through what Linkedin is and how to use it at:
http://www.youtube.com/user/LinkedinMarketing

Linkedin on Twitter

Everyone seems to be on Twitter these days and if you want to keep up with what's happening with Linkedin then you can follow their tweets at: http://twitter.com/Linkedin

Personal Branding

If you want to know more about Personal Branding in general, then I suggest you check out Dan Scwabel's blog at http://www.personalbrandingblog.com.

INDEX

Lightning Source UK Ltd.
Milton Keynes UK
UKOW031501300412

191747UK00007B/12/P